Book 6:

Almost Grown Up...

Clarissa and Gregory

Written and Illustrated by

Nadine Redfield

ISBN: 978-1-958407-40-0 (hardback)

ISBN: 978-1-958407-41-7 (soft cover)

WWW.ELMGROVEPUBLISHING.COM
San Antonio, Texas
Book design by: designpanache

Book 6:

Almost Grown Up...

Clarissa
and Gregory

Meet Clarissa and Gregory

Clarissa and Gregory are real children, a brother and sister who lived in America a long time ago, long before there were cell phones or computers or even television.

They had lots of adventures together!

Some of their adventures are very funny. And some of them are very scary!

When Gregory grew up, he worked for National Cash Register. Clarissa worked as a seamstress, but she was an artist who also liked to write, and many years later, she wrote this series of books about growing up in rural Michigan in the 1920s and '30s and into World War Two!

Contents

Dedicated to the memory of my dear brother,
Paul Gregory, who lived these adventures with me.

Clarissa and Gregory.
Clayton, Michigan, 1929

Baby Roosters

"Clarissa, this summer while you are out of school you could raise some baby chicks and sell them to earn some spending money," Mama told her.

"I would love to do that," Clarissa replied thinking how fun it was to play with fuzzy little chicks.

"We'll get little roosters because the little hen chicks are sold first and are more expensive. The farmers buy them, because when they grow into hens they lay eggs to sell.

The next time they went to town, Mama took Clarissa to the nursery where they put fertile eggs in warm incubators for 24 days and little baby chicks hatch out of the eggs.

At the nursery, the whole building was alive with the sound of hundreds of baby chicks cheeping.

"We want to buy a dozen baby roosters," Clarissa said proudly to the man behind the counter.

"I'll loan you the money to buy the baby chicks and the feed. You can pay me back when we sell them," Mama told her.

On the way home in the car, Clarissa held the box of baby chicks in her lap. The box had round holes all along the sides, to let in air so the little chicks could breathe.

"The chicks are so fuzzy," Clarissa told her Mama while poking her finger through the holes to pet the little yellow babies.

"They sure are noisy."

"They're hungry. When we get them home we'll feed them, and give them some water to drink. They need to be kept warm until they start to grow feathers. We'll keep them in the basement while they are little," Mama instructed her.

At home, Clarissa put some newspapers on the floor in the basement near the warm cook stove. She put some feed in an old pie tin, and laid it on the papers. She gently lifted the soft baby chicks out of their box. They went straight to the feed and started to eat.

"Clarissa, they need water to drink. Here is an old watering jar we can use," Mama told her.

Clarissa watched her Mama pour the water into the metal jar. It was made out of blue-gray galvanized tin with a top that screwed onto a wider round pan like a bowl. This made a place for the water to run down for the chicks to drink when the jar was turned upside down.

"Thank you Mama. Next time I'll know how to give them water," Clarissa said picking up the watering can, and placing it on the papers.

The baby chicks ran to the water and started to drink. They dipped their little beaks in the water and raised their heads up high as if to say a thank you prayer each time they drank.

"Time for a nap, little chicks," Clarissa told her babies as she gathered them up into a large box Mama had given her. It had more papers lined in the bottom. Mama gave her an old towel to put over the top of the box to keep them warm.

Daddy built them a little house. Then Clarissa moved the chicks outside when the weather was warmer. They ran loose in the yard during the day, and at night they went into the house to sleep. Clarissa made sure the door was closed tightly once they were safe inside.

Clarissa took care of the chicks all summer, watching them grow feathers and learn to crow. She laughed at their funny little crowing noises. They certainly didn't crow like a big rooster.

One day after school, Clarissa came home from school, and Mama told her. "I sold your roosters today to Cousin Myron."

"How much did you get for them?" Clarissa asked eagerly.

"You made $5.00 but remember the cost of the chicks, and the feed?" Mama reminded her.

"Here are the receipts for the chicks and the feed. Let's add them up – the cost comes to $5.29. You don't have to pay me the 29 cents," Mama told her.

"You mean I didn't make any money after taking care of them all summer? How does Cousin Charlotte make money when she sells her chickens?" Clarissa asked sadly.

"It is because she doesn't have to buy the feed. She uses grain that her father raises on their farm." Mama told her.

"I am so disappointed. I am never going to raise little roosters again. I wish we lived on a farm so I wouldn't have to buy feed," Clarissa said holding back the tears. She tried to remember all the fun it was watching the little chicks grow and learn to crow, even if she didn't earn any money.

Two Little Pigs

It was summertime again and school was out. Mama wanted to keep Clarissa busy.

"Daddy told me a farmer has only two baby pigs and doesn't want to raise just the two of them. He wants to know if you would like to raise them. You can give them milk from Donna Boss, our cow," Mama said.

"It will be fun to have two little pigs to play with this summer. I won't have to buy milk to feed them so maybe I can make some money this time," Clarissa said.

Daddy brought the two wiggly little piglets home and carried them to the basement in a tan gunny sack. They were squealing loudly when Clarissa lifted the piglets out of the sack.

"Oh, one is black and the other one is white with black spots. I won't have any trouble telling them apart, Clarissa explained.

"The black one is a boy and the other one is a girl," Mama told her.

"I'll name them Jack and Jill," Clarissa said with pride for her new little family of piglets.

"Tomorrow I'll make you a trough for their milk so you can feed your little pigs," Daddy explained.

"Clarissa here is some milk for the little pigs in this deep pan. We'll clean out the little building you used for the roosters last summer, and they can sleep in there," Mama explained.

"Oh, Daddy this trough is so cute, and just the right size for the little pigs. It looks just like the big ones. Thank you," Clarissa told her Daddy.

All summer, Clarissa fed the little pigs each morning, and again in the evening after Mama had milked Donna Boss. Sometimes the little piglets got hungry before it was time for Mama to milk her cow. The pig-lets thought Clarissa was their mother so they chased her around the yard squealing loudly. When they caught her they rubbed their little cold noses on her legs to tell her they were hungry.

One day Mama was late getting home from town, and the little pigs were hungry. Clarissa knew she had to find a way to feed them so she got a pail and decided she had to try to milk Donna Boss. She had never milked sweet Donna Boss before, but her babies were hungry and needed some milk.

Clarissa got the milking pail and walked over to the cow, sat down on Mama's three legged stool and started to milk her. At first nothing hap-pened, but before long she got the hang of it and was able to get enough milk to feed her baby pigs until Mama got home.

"Thank you, Donna Boss for the milk. The little pigs will be happy now when I give them some milk," Clarissa said to the family cow.

It was about time for school to start, and the little pigs were ready to be sold. No longer could they live on milk alone. They needed feed to eat.

Mama found a man to buy the pigs, but he told her that they were small and he would have to fatten them up with feed before he could sell them. I'll give you $2.50 a piece for them.

Mama counted out the money to Clarissa.

"Is that all I got for all my work all summer, Mama?" questioned Clarissa.

"The man said that they were too small to pay more than that for them," Mama told her.

Clarissa reached for the money, and was glad to get it, for little girls always need money to buy birthday presents and special school supplies.

"It isn't profitable to raise little pigs or little roosters, and I'll never do that again. How do farmers make any money?" Clarissa wondered.

Growing Cucumbers to Make Pickles

The next summer Mama had another idea for Clarissa to make some spending money.

"Clarissa how would you like to raise some cucumbers to pick and sell to the pickle factory in town?" Mama asked her.

"I guess I could. Maybe I'll make lots of money this time. I didn't make much money raising little roosters or little pigs," Clarissa told her Mama, not very excited about all the back-breaking work it would take, but she did need some spending money. She was going to start Junior High School in town in the fall, so she needed some new clothes.

"You can use the small garden. Daddy will get Uncle Ray and his mules to plow it up for you. Then we can plant the seeds," Mama told her.

Clarissa watched Uncle Ray plow up the garden with his two mules, named Rex and Ginny, harnessed to the plow. He went up and down the garden until all the dirt in the garden was plowed.

Mama grabbed a rake and started to level the dirt.

"Clarissa there is another rake in the barn for you to use.

When the ground is leveled we'll make mounds to plant the seeds on. I have plenty of seeds that I saved from last year. We won't have to buy any," Mama told her all excited.

Clarissa went to the barn and got the rake and started working with the dirt.

"This is hard work, and we'll never get all this ground leveled," Clarissa told her mother, wondering why her Mama loved digging in the dirt so much. It didn't seem like fun to her and it made her back hurt.

"Mama, I am so tired. Can I do this tomorrow?" Clarissa asked her Mother. "Aren't you tired too?"

"You can go and rest," Mama told her not looking up from her work.

"I am going in the house now," Clarissa told her feeling guilty seeing her Mama work so hard. Her body just wasn't strong enough to do all this hard work yet.

"Why do you plant the seeds on the mounds, Mama," Clarissa asked.

"It is because the plants send out runners for the cucumbers to grow on. The ground will be covered with runners before long," Mama told her.

With Mama's help the seeds got planted on the mounds. Five seeds went into each mound, then Clarissa covered the seeds with soft dirt.

"You have to be careful not to step on the runners when you pick the cucumbers. After a nice rain the seeds will send up little green shoots. Next, the vines will appear, and they will spring out in every direction on the mounds," Mama explained.

One nice warm morning Clarissa was still asleep when her Mama came into her bedroom all excited.

"Clarissa, the vines are all in bloom and you'll have some little cucumbers soon. I am pulling weeds. Get dressed, then come and help me. This is a beautiful morning," Mama told her.

"The little blossoms are sort of cute. How long before they will turn into little pickles?" Clarissa asked pulling some weeds.

"They won't be pickles yet. They are cucumbers until they are made into pickles. When the petals fall off, tiny little cucumbers will form. They grow fast so it won't be long now," Mama told her.

"I can hardly wait for them to be big enough to pick. Cousin Charlotte told me that she can take me to town when she goes to take her pickles–I mean cucumbers–to the pickle factory," Clarissa said.

Clarissa watched the little cucumbers appear and grow big enough to pick. The vines and little leaves had fuzz on them. It hurt her fingers if she wasn't careful. At first there weren't enough cucumbers to sell so Mama made a cucumber and onion salad with water, vinegar, salt and pepper. She served the salad in a brown and white crock.

After a while there were enough cucumbers to pick to sell. They couldn't be picked until the wet dew had cleared off the vines. The cucumbers needed to be picked every other day. Clarissa picked two small sacks full. The small cucumbers two inches or less went into one sack, and the larger ones went into another sack. Sometimes the cucumbers hid under leaves, and she missed them. When they grew too big they turned yellow and had to be thrown away. This made Clarissa sad when she had to throw them away.

Charlotte told Clarissa that she would be there soon to pick her up and deliver the cucumbers to the pickle factory. When Charlotte arrived, Clarissa saw all the sacks she had in the back seat.

"How come you have so many sacks of cucumbers Charlotte?" Clarissa asked thinking that her cousin was 10 years older than her.

"I have a large patch of cucumbers, and it takes a long time to pick them all. It is larger than your garden," Charlotte explained.

"It takes me a long time to pick my cucumbers, and I am glad my garden isn't any larger than it is," Clarissa told her. When they arrived at the pickle factory, Cousin Ed met them to help Charlotte carry her sacks to the scales. Clarissa carried her own because they weren't very heavy.

"These are the small ones and these are the large ones," Charlotte explained.

Cousin Ed weighed them and took the sacks to a very large wooden barrel, and dumped them into the smelly brine. He handed Charlotte some paper money which she folded up, and some coins.

"Now we will weigh yours, Clarissa. For the small ones you get more money per pound than you get for the large ones, he told her.

Clarissa watched him weigh her little sacks then he handed her some coins, but no paper money. "That is a lot of work for so little money," she thought.

All summer Clarissa saved her money, but she never did get any paper money to fold up. She was always paid in coins, but she was faithful, and saved it all. She didn't even spend any of it for a popsicle on the way home, even though Charlotte sometimes bought one and shared it with her. Charlotte seemed to always have lots of money in her purse.

"I hope when I am older I will have lots of money in my purse like Charlotte," Clarissa thought.

One day the Sears Roebuck catalog came in the mailbox. Clarissa was so excited looking through the catalog, dreaming of how she would spend her money. She wanted to buy some new clothes for school.

After studying the catalog very hard, she decided on a warm camel colored coat, a print dress and a pair of brown shoes. With Mama's help the order was mailed. Then she waited for the mailman to deliver the box of clothes.

"Mama, I didn't get much money for all the work I did all summer. Why do you like working in your garden so much?" Clarissa asked.

"I love to work in my garden because the land was given to us by your grandmother, and I am thankful for that. Then the precious little seeds are put into the ground, then God sends us the sunshine and rain. The seeds grow, and the plants make vegetables for me to pick so I can feed my family," Mama explained.

"That is so much work, Mama. I hate to see you work so hard," Clarissa said.

"It isn't work to me because all the time I am working I am thinking of the vegetables we have to eat all summer, then I put the vegetables in cans for us to eat in the winter," Mama told her.

"You must love us very much," Clarissa told her mother, thinking that working in the ground raising vegetables wasn't the way she wanted to spend her life.

Finally the package came with the coat, the dress, and the shoes. Clarissa opened the box. She tried on everything and it all fit perfectly. She was so thrilled and proud of her purchases.

"Mama, I love my new clothes, my coat will keep me nice and warm this winter. This is the first store-bought coat I have ever had!"

Clarissa was happy but still she thought, "There must be a better way to make money than to raise little roosters, little pigs or grow pickles–I mean cucumbers."

"When I grow up I am going to get a job in the big city, and marry a tall dark, and handsome man who is *not* a farmer!"

And that is exactly what she did!

The Mean Cow

"I just love summer evenings. Mama has already milked the cows, so we'll have supper early tonight," Clarissa told Gregory.

"Yeah, and, I told Dad that we would take the cows to pasture," Gregory said.

Since they didn't live on a farm with a meadow, like Uncle Ray, the cows were chained to stakes driven into the ground. They ate grass from around the circle where they were staked. So when the grass was eaten up, a new place was found with fresh grass.

"Gregory, the cows need to have their stakes changed for fresh grass. Don't forget to take the mallet with you," Daddy called. A mallet is a large hammer-like tool with a long handle and a barrel shaped head used for driving stakes into the ground.

"OK. Here, take Donna Boss's chain, and I'll walk mean ol' Mutt," Gregory told Clarissa, putting the heavy mallet over his shoulder while holding on to Mutt's chain with the other hand.

Donna Boss was the first cow, and the family loved her as a pet, but

the new cow was something else.

"I wonder why Mutt doesn't like women and children," Clarissa asked. "Yesterday she put her head down, and started running toward our neighbor, Mrs. Wheeler, and her two children, Leona and Alvin. They came over when the cows were at the well getting a drink."

"Mama had to grab Mutt's chain so she wouldn't charge them," Gregory said.

"At first Mutt tried to do that to Mama, but she let the cow know right away that she wasn't going to put up with her antics.

"You hit Mutt with a stick once, and she never bothered you after that. I am still afraid of her. Hang on tight so she won't run after me," Clarissa said.

"Now that Mama has two cows, she has more milk, butter and cottage cheese to sell," Gregory added.

"Donna Boss is such a sweet and gentle cow. She is a Guernsey cow, and I think she is beautiful. She gives more milk than ol' Mutt, who is a Jersey cow," Clarissa said, petting Donna Boss on the side of her head.

Gregory put down Mutt's chain to drive the stake into the ground so she would have nice fresh grass. When ol' Mutt realized she was free, she put her head down and started running toward Clarissa.

Clarissa was terrified. She knew she had nowhere to go in the open field. What should she do? She knew she couldn't outrun Mutt. Fear gripped her, and her heart pounded madly. Suddenly, she had an idea. Clarissa started jumping up and down, waving her arms and making strange noises. Mutt was a coward, and didn't want to approach such a strange-acting character. Mutt put on the brakes and stopped dead in her tracks.

"I have her chain now, Clarissa. She can't hurt you," Gregory called to his sister.

"I sure am glad you have Mutt's chain. I was so afraid for a while." Clarissa frowned, then turned and stared into Mutt's eyes, and told her, "Ol' Mutt you sure are a mean cow. Why can't you be sweet like Donna Boss?"

"It won't do any good to scold her, Clarissa. She'll never change."

"Yeah, some people are just mean and miserable."

"She is like that mean ol' man that didn't want to pay Dad for the lumber he sawed for him," Gregory said.

"Well, I would rather be like Donna Boss. Sweet, kind, and happy."

"Yeah, she sure is a contented cow," Gregory added.

Picking Strawberries for Jam with a Snake!

Every year Clarissa helped her mother make strawberry jam but this year Mama hadn't made any. It was getting late in the season for strawberries. Clarissa though that her family wouldn't have any strawberry jam for Mama's hot biscuits if she didn't make some jam.

"Mama, can I make some strawberry jam? We have enough sugar (sugar was rationed during the war) and some pectin to make it jell. I can pick a couple quarts of strawberries in the strawberry patch. I watched you make jam so I think I can do it," Clarissa told her mother.

"That would be nice. Since the war is on I am working and I don't have time to do a lot of things that I used to do. Your Dad is working at the sawmill in Ohio, so I don't cook much anymore," Mama told Clarissa.

"I'll go out to the strawberry patch and pick some berries. I hope I can find enough to make jam," Clarissa told her mother, feeling a little sad that things weren't like they used to be.

World War Two was raging overseas. Farmers went to work in the war factories, and some of their wives also went to work. Young men went off to fight in the war.

Sugar was rationed, and so were shoes. Stamps had to be used when you bought certain things. When the stamps were used up, people had to do without. Everyone was allowed three pairs of shoes in a year, but in her whole life, Clarissa had never had three pairs of shoes in one year. She was lucky if she had two pairs of shoes in a year. Now that people were working, they had more money to buy things that they couldn't afford during the Great Depression. The problem was that all the factories were making things for the war. No new cars, washing machines, tires or a lot of other things were manufactured during the war. Old things just had to do or be fixed.

It was quite a walk to the strawberry patch. The strawberries were planted on a long strip between the hay field and the corn field.

"I think I'll start at the far end, and work toward the house," Clarissa reasoned, carrying two square, wooden quart baskets.

Clarissa hoped she could find enough red strawberries to fill her baskets. The plants were tired from making berries all summer. Mama hadn't gone near the strawberry patch in a long time since she was working.

"Oh, I see lots of red berries! I think I can find enough!" Clarissa thought. She picked one basket full then started filling the second one.

"Oh, help!" Clarissa let out a loud scream when she heard a slithering noise. She looked in the direction of the sound and saw a huge black racer snake. Her heart started pounding so hard, it almost burst! She wanted to run home, even though she knew black racer snakes were harmless.

"I am going to finish picking enough strawberries to fill this bas-

ket even though I'm afraid. If I scream once in awhile, maybe I'll scare the snake away," Clarissa told herself, knowing nobody could hear her scream so far from the house.

She heard the snake once more up ahead, slithering on the ground, but Clarissa kept picking the strawberries until she both baskets were full.

Back home, Clarissa washed the two quarts of precious berries, then removed the stems and leaves. She gathered up seven small jars, and washed them with soapy water. Next, she carefully poured boiling hot water in the jars to kill any germs they might have. She took a pan, put in the berries, mashed them, and added sugar.

Since electricity was now wired into their house, the family had a kitchen built on the back, conplete with an electric stove. No longer did they have the old wooden cook stove in the basement. She turned the heat on the stove and started cooking the berries.

"I am so glad we have an electric stove now so I don't have to build a fire in the old cook stove," Clarissa thought.

On the box of pectin she read the instructions that told her when to add it to the boiling berries. She followed the instructions carefully. Every now and then Clarissa skimmed off the white froth that formed. She didn't know why, but Mama always did this.

When the red strawberries were cooked just right, she added the pectin then poured the hot mixture into the waiting jars. She had enough jam left over to put in a bowl for supper, for when Mama made hot biscuits. When the jars of jam had cooled a little she melted some paraffin wax and poured it over the top of the jars. This sealed in the jam to keep it from spoiling. She was pleased, and hoped Mama would be happy too.

"I am so glad I stayed and picked enough strawberries to make the jam. Even though I was afraid of the snake," Clarissa thought.

Mama and Clarissa enjoyed hot biscuits with the jam for supper that night, and had strawberry jam all winter long!

The End

www.ingramcontent.com/pod-product-compliance
Lightning Source LLC
Chambersburg PA
CBHW041132120626
46547CB00019B/2962